The Scoundrel of Saigon
Mister. E

ISBN
Printed, Distributed and Bound in the United
States of America First Printing
April 2022
Published by He Who Rebels Against All

You would think eye would be exhausted after writing (and selling) 17 books in under three years.

Not remotely.

While the rest of the world works remotely during the pandemic,

I have been typing up a syntactical storm.

The political winds are quickly shifting and I

have been given my 2nd wind.

The sustained, cumulative shocks to the system and the tides of history moving, have become shocks to my system.

The realization that this is a historical moment.

Books of the past are falling off the shelves, the shelves themselves are shaking and wobbling.

Words from others wont matter.

Might not even be remembered.

Im climbing up, as the world and literary world crumble.

To the Yunnan province, To Lijiang, to Jinsha, To Jade Dragon snow mountains, to the Qingyi river, to suzhou, to HongKong,

Back To Lijang,

TO Wulingyuan, to Jiuzhaigou,

To XI'an, to Beijing

I descend from the western territory of The
United States.

To the markets of Manchu

*dons rice farmer hat, brick stomping sandals,
and tucks my gun into my shirt*

Let's roll,
Eggroll.

I am the scoundrel of Saigon,
After the Weasel of Wuhan.

We enter an empire, much older than america,
with a history much richer,
and food much better than your local
Mcdonalds.

This is a land of historical turning points,
Of dynasty and ambition, technological power,
with economic might.

Political insanity, mixed with Fried rice.

This is the land of the Blessed Panda.

A land of war, blood, pain, strife, and splendor.

Golden Lotus,
Bloody Revolutions.

This is The land Donald Trump over-enunciated
and called CHYyy-NUH, while equally
underestimating their skill, chessmanship,
statesmanship and cunning.

Make no mistake, for all the asian/Oriental jokes out there.

China and it's people are no joke.

Skilled, intelligent, proficient.

Leagues above the fat american kid crying for an Ipad.

China is making the parts for your fat american kid to have the ipad, to begin with.

Technological, Academic, Military minded, state obedient.

This is a different stock of people, riding the wings on the winds of history.

If Americans are slow and angry,
Russians (not much different, just more brutish)
from bear to polar bear

The Panda land is a people of quiet determination.

It Isn't only a stereotype that asians are smart.

They actually, simply are.

So, listen up, smart asses
because you think you know everything.

You dont know jack about what Xhinese Jill is capable of.

They are a people of the eastern fox, the rabbit, the monkey, and the dragon,
And a people equally enslaved to their government agencies, in ways far worse than

americans can ever conceive.

If you call Joe biden "stupid" in america, you get 300 thumbs up.

If you call Xi Jinping "stupid" in China, you can get life in prison.

Or killed.

Different judicial strokes for different ethnic folks.

*speeds through the markets of Hong Kong on a moped, and disappears in the crowd with a dragon motorscycle white helmet.

Chapter 2

I realized literary acclaim, and scholastic,
literary achievement mattered very little to me.

I had cast off those ambitions and gone full
journalist,
after spending years entrenched in medical
and science journals.

I was still writing, but not...really... writing

books.

Reports.

And reporting on unfolding events.

I tell people I'm a writer, but the truth is,
I'm a full print-to-paper journalist, these days.

I can't wait around for months to years to
publish.

It has to be right now.

There is an urgency that the traditional literary
process cannot accommodate or assist.

We have to do this. RIGHT. NOW.

Now the truth.

I extended my print run and kept writing books -

only to get further into the case of covid-19.

I was writing filler material, JUST to keep my name circulating.

I learned an invaluable lesson.

People don't actually care what you've written.

They're more impressed by sales certificates and seeing your name on google.

I could write absolute trash, total literary junk, and it wouldn't matter.

Not anymore.

Because people aren't reading.

What they're reading is social media, tiktok, and snapchat messages.

Books are long dead.

Not yet long gone.

But dead as dead gets.

And they're not coming back.

And that meant information proliferation would also have to change.

to keep up with culture.

Stops at a chinese warehouse, lockpicks the door, looks around the alley as chinese flags wave in the wind, and slowly pushes the door in

Come on, we have some things to get, here.

The four horsemen of the apocalypse are engraved in the wood paneling.

We need some supplies / to fight all the lies.

throws you the keys

Hold those for me

grabs bundled chinese scrolls, Ammunition, Antiviral pills and injections and A framed photo of Fauci

a social scientist must be the one to intellectually take on and take down a medical scientist.

sociologist vs. sociopath.

turns the lights out in the chinese warehouse, relocks the door and gets back on the bike

Let's get this show on the road, before the final showdown.

Come oN!

revs the engine of the motorscycle

Hold on, we've got to get to Wuhan.

speeds through the streets as driver's honk

Chapter 3

I've got to tell you the truth of some things before we get there.

One, I was using literature to get closer to the story of the Wuhan Institute of Virology.

I used my entire print run, name, reputation to build credentials, just to get to the epicenter where all this began

accelerates through the Gangzhou highway

I was a nobody before this. like a total nobody. before i became somebody.

Before my books went international,
I was a struggling indie writer, with the only success I saw was local coffee shops selling my work.

I never saw any international exposure until I wrote about covid19. and sold it to international markets.

it was seductive to see my name climb up charts, and sell in target and walmart.

I wont lie.

But that wasnt enough for me.

I knew I had the story of my career.

I knew covid19 wasnt just going to change the world,
I knew It was going to change mine.

flashbacks

Before We got all the way out here,

I had written one book and had decent exposure that drew moderate attention to my name. I then knew I had the chance of drawing it out.

I am an artist of deception, darling.

And i've made it this far.

I was thirsty for more, after my first novel was published.

The editorial team I was working with, was waiting for anything big to break... and then... like magic.... Covid-19 happened.

Overnight, the world changed and went into restrictive shutdowns and lockdowns.

On the editorial board was a thumb-tacked notecard that read "new virus."

I wanted that story.

I was going to get that story.

Another writer was poised, originally, to cover it.

He chickened out because of the fear of speaking about china and being perceived as racist.

I wasn't scared of shit.

zig-zags through six cars in the lanes next to us

speeds up

hold on

Within three months of the pandemic's start, I had written the first novel *kong flu panda* and sold it to retail stores around the world.

I had seeded my first, big hit.

And I also knew, while literary success was starting to take off, there were enough lies happening regarding the origins of covid19, to start to build a case.

Even if I had to go against liberal, nutjobs.

And I did.

revs engine

Chapter 4

But I had my own shady reasons.

Well not shady to me, but shady to people with morals.

Lmao.

Whenever i needed access, to databases I couldnt get inside, to science journals I couldn't read,

I just flashed my books and showed them a link to the retailers.

It opened doors. Without question.

It was like a cop flashing a badge.

I was totally unqualified to get access to some of the information I acquired, screenshotted and took.

But people are amazed by anything.

my print run gave me everything I needed, as well as a run for the money.

I was running it all, through smoke and mirrors.

I needed to get closer to the origins.

And the only way to do it, was to inflate my identity on the landscape.

And it worked.

Dont be mad now, I already got all the information I needed.

If fauci is the weasel of wuhan,
I am the scoundrel of saigon.

And these lab notes are gonna be gone with the wind, if we dont get there in time.

That was the thing.

Timing.

Deep down, i had wanted to take a break.

A long one.

I wanted to disappear for years.

Other artists, writers and literary "kind" do it, all the time.

But the thing was this.

Information was rapidly being deleted, hidden, tucked away, and moved around.

I definitely couldnt take a break or a breather for years, not even months.

What i needed would be scrubbed clean, by then.

That is the scariest part of all of this.

It's not the pathogen.

it's not the depopulation.
It's not even the destabalization that's
happened.

It's the muddying the waters of information and
how information access is being manipulated.

We're not talking government secret, classified
information.

We're talking google, basic search index
information.

It's all being controlled now.

By tech and the state.

Is Americxa really different from Xhina?

Not by much.

Not anymore.

Not after Trump let russia stick three fingers
in our ass,
and China finger lady liberty's private parts.

we're fucked.

We've been fucked.

I know it's just now setting in.

we're cumming in Kunming.

+ We're about to arrive in Huanggang,

Get ready for a 4way chinese gang bang.

Hubei, baybay.

NIH grants signed by Fauci fly back in the wind as the motorsycle speeds on

I am the scoundrel of Saigon, Motherfucker.